BE AN OWNER
Stop Renting Your Life

J E R E M Y   B R O O K S

Steward Publishing, LTD.

🌐 stewardpublishing.org

Table of Contents

Dedication 5

Foreword 7

Introduction 13

Chapter 1 21

Chapter 2 29

Chapter 3 35

Chapter 4 41

Chapter 5 51

Chapter 6 79

Chapter 7 87

Chapter 8 91

Chapter 9 97

Acknowledgments 103

Dedication

First, I would like to dedicate this book to my beautiful wife for keeping my brain clear while creating this book. She is my backbone and I can't do it without her part. My kids I love you guys from the moon and back.

I would also like to dedicate this to my mother Doris Brooks and father, David Brooks. These two incredible people are like flowers and water, different in every way but the one thing they can agree on is the love for each other. If you cut me in half one side is my mother creative and professional character. On the other side I have my father work ethic and drive. Love you both.

Next, I would like to dedicate my book to the city of Detroit "313" that taught me how to survive this crazy world as a young boy. Best city in the world. No debate needed.

Lastly, I would also like to dedicate my book to CAU Clark Atlanta University who taught me the motto "I'll Find a Way or Make One." I live up to this motto every-day of my life.

Foreword

By: Dr. Chauna D. Everett

It can be said that behind every successful man there is a good woman. My brother is no exception to this rule and his beautiful wife Tenesha is a great example. She stands behind him, as he tries to take over the world. Many years before Jeremy met the love of his life, he had a big sister that held this sacred role. Now don't get me wrong, I am definitely not the hand holding, wipe your running nose, and go scare the Boogie man type of big sister. I was more of what you would call a motivational support. How can I put this, have you ever seen the show Survivor? Well close your eyes and imagine a 1981 version of the show but only one person knows they are playing. That one player with the knowledge of said game was the 6 year old girl looking down into her little brother's bassinet.

Much like the television show, each contestant's goal was to "outwit, outplay, and outlast" other contestants to become the *Soul Survivor*. We didn't have a secluded island or a network filming crew but man did we have a 5 bedroom brick house in the middle of Detroit's Northwest neighborhood. Our older sister, my brother and I grew up in a middle class neighborhood and we watched our parents work hard for the"American Dream". Our father worked his way from the mailroom at EDS to a corporate position within General Motors. Our mother was a claims adjuster by day but by night she was like a superhero, and there was nothing she was afraid to pursue.

I guess you can say Jeremy is a great mix of our parents. He got his work ethic from our dad and fearless ambition from our mother. All he was missing was a catalyst to teach him to "outwit, outplay, and outlast", that's where I came in. I remember Jeremy coming home from school when he was 10 concerned that his cub scout group was going to be sleeping in the woods and he wasn't going to go. As his big sister it was my job to make sure he didn't give into his fears. So as loving as possible, I reminded him of the times I locked him in closets, pushed him down the stairs in the laundry basket ect and he lived through it all. Knowing that he was not completely sold on sleeping outside at night, I decided to put a cherry on top by giving him some pearls of wisdom. I told him "you can make money while you are there." His little eyes lit up as I further explained how he could take extra candy and snacks to sell while he was there. Thank goodness our mother was ahead of the curve and bought in bulk, so supply was not an issue. Needless to say, the demand was already built in with limited snack access and target audience, Jeremy sold out of his entire stash.

As I would love to take credit for my brother's success, I cannot. He had an entrepreneurial spirit that started early and maintained throughout his life. In high school he was reading *Rich Dad Poor Dad* when most of his friends were barely reading the required material for class. This was the same time he had a full on"convenience store" in his locker and was Uber before there was Uber. Jeremy was never a follower as a teenager and that continued until throughout his adult life. Returning from practicing medicine in New York, I can't tell you what job my brother had at the time, but what I do remember is him still having a fire in his belly to own a business.

In 2011, Jeremy came down to North Carolina. I watched him create a lifestyle with multiple streams of income and generational wealth for his family. Writing this book seems like a natural progression to solidify his success. This book is more than a "How to..", it is truly a blueprint to be successful in business. He gives a transparent look into the good, the bad, and the ugly. As the wife of a business owner, we have taken the principles in this book to grow our transportation company. I am honored to write the forward for this book and not because he is my brother but because this book is needed now more than ever. One might say that the "student has more than become the teacher!"

"Success is only meaningful and enjoyable if it feels like your own"

— Michelle Obama

Introduction

"It was all a dream"

You have to ask yourself the million-dollar question "Why?" or "What?". Why are you thinking about becoming an owner? What is your motivation for pursuing a life changing action? In fact, exactly 20% of new businesses fail in the first two years. Now, don't get discouraged because I want you to fall in the 80% of successful business owners.

But again, you have to ask the question. What is my motivation? Write it down on a sticky note place it on the mirror in your bathroom. This should be the first thing you see in the morning. Place another sticky note in your car so you can see it on your way to and from work. Lastly, place one on your laptop or desktop computer for when the late night, researching takes a toll. When you feel like quitting look at the sticky note for motivation.

A lot of people motivations are very different. One of the biggest motivations people have in common is one word, which is "money". Money controls your every move in business and mainly in your life. It tells you where you are going to live and what bills are going to get paid that week. One thing everyone in the world has the same reaction to is their bank account.

Either you don't have enough or you're loaded and have too much money.

I am going to guide you to fall somewhere in the middle. Growing your business so you have that too much "money" in the bank feeling.

People I meet everyday ask me what is my motivation? This is a very easy question to answer but over the years my answer have changed. As a teenager, my motivation was cloudy. I knew I wanted to own a business but didn't have the drive to run it. All I wanted was something of my own and money in the bank. Growing up in Detroit, the city was known for hustling and gators. Detroit is a very blue-collar hard, working city that will support all young entrepreneurs and a true side hustle. I had a saying just like New York is the concrete jungle, Detroit is an entrepreneur and side hustlers' playground if your business makes it there it will make it anywhere. I had the blessing to be around some incredible business owners and hustlers who without knowing taught me the good bad, and ugly in business. Close your eyes, picture a young ambitious man who was a sponge willing to learn everything in one day. Never really having the guidance and mentor to build a business at a young age. Once again my vision was cloudy but motivation was there to take on anything that came my way. I thought I could try to take over the world as I say this in my pinky and brain voice. Sorry for the 90's Animaniacs throwback I'm a geek I know.

But now in this present time my motivation is totally different. I am in a different mindset I think like a provider, like a leader not a selfish human being. The only things that motivate me are my kids and money. Yes, money is still a factor. It's a factor because I want to make sure my kids and their kids have generational wealth they can benefit from, from the start of their own businesses. So, again ask yourself "Why?" or "What?" motivates you. Close your eyes try to visualize motivation then write it down. The freedom of owner-ship and generational wealth starts with the person who hates being told what to do and is sick of renting their life. Time to be an owner.

What is blocking your vision?   But, be honest with yourself write down the truth.

_____

_____

_____

_____

_____

_____

_____

_____

_____

_____

_____

_____

_____

_____

_____

_____

_____

_____

_____

_____

_____

_____

_____

_____

_____

_____

_____

_____

_____

"I'm living everyday like a hustle, another drug to juggle. Another day, another struggle"

— *Biggie Smalls*

Chapter 1

"People start a business everyday! You will be alright your tough" Right!

Athletes will lift weights and drink protein shakes everyday in the pursuit of domination to reach championship level. Entrepreneurs and side hustle warriors have to train the same way. When you decide to enter yourself into the draft of ownership you are the star on your team, number one draft pick, a leader looking for domination and commander of your life.

So, you may ask yourself, how do I train my mind like an athlete? Like most athletes you have to clean your mind from toxic thoughts and feelings. This starts with the people you are around on a daily basis. Always associate yourself with people who have the same mind set as you. Sitting and not moving will not build that mind muscle. When you talk to people who have the same mind set or who is training their mind like you things in your head start to change. Your vision will start to be clearer and your mind will start to build what I call "grind muscle". Grind muscle will allow you to be up all night researching for business and outlining what needs to be done. This is when you know the first step of ownership has started.

Back to talking about toxic people, here are a couple of good examples that will help you define, or pen point people who are not on your side. We are going to look at a fictional story but word for word what entrepreneurs and side hustle warriors have to deal with.

Let's meet Stacy...She is a college graduate and a single mother of three children with one in college. She works a 9 to 5 at a law firm as a paralegal making just ok money. She makes enough that her bills are getting paid, but with no money left over. Stacy has been at this job for 7 years doing the same thing everyday. Well, one day Stacy had to interview a young man named Alex. Alex is a newly college graduate working on getting into law school. In fact, the young man went to the same college Stacy's daughter goes to. So, after the formal interview Stacy asks Alex, "What do you like to do outside of work? Let me guess "party" (they both laugh)". He said, "no, I am working on my business I'm a professional photographer." Stacy was shocked at his answer and looked very interested. She always wanted to start her own business but was too scared to do so.

She went home and thought about it all night. She finally decided that helping people is her passion so that's what she is going to do. Stacy was so excited about her new business idea she wanted to tell every-one. So, she had lunch with her childhood friend Mary the next day. Stacy and Mary sat down and as they started laughing and eating Stacy said, "I have decided to start my own business helping young girls." Then Mary says, "What? Why? You will not make any money." Mary also decides to say "when will

we have time to hangout, don't waste your time and money, most businesses fail anyway."

Stacy went from being on top of the world to low and dirty. She allowed her friend to poison her mind with negativity and fear. This example was to show you guys that people can break your spirits just by asking "why?" So as an entrepreneur and side hustle warrior, you need to put on that hater blocker just like sunglasses. Block the noise and focus on your training.

Now, the second example is a little different scenario look at how Alex started his business. Alex is a college student who had an eye for photography. He has always talked to his cousin about starting a photography business as a side hustle. But the main reason Alex didn't start his business and second-guessing himself is because he thinks a broke college student will not be able to afford to start a business. One day Alex went to his cousin house to talk and just see how he was doing. Alex's cousin asks him how is the start of the business going? Alex takes a deep breath and says, "it's not going anywhere." His cousin says, "what is the issue?" His cousin looks at him and says, "let me be your partner in business so we can get it started." So, then Alex and his cousin goes out and buys everything he needs.

This shows you that one person can change your whole outlook to start a business. With support and guidance in Alex's case he gained a partner in business.

When I talk to new or veteran entrepreneurs and side hustle warriors, I always tell them never let anyone control your mind. You should have the first and last decision when starting or running your own business. I want you to write down the things that are clouding your brain. These are the things that will stop your vision. Don't be surprised what's clouding your vision maybe you. I heard a quote from a young entrepreneur, a true side hustle warrior who started a street nacho business on the streets of Baltimore. He said, "Your fortune is in your daily routine." Think about that for a minute "your fortune is in your daily routine." Powerful statement he said, "I'm on IG every day first thing in the morning." When he saw someone making nachos, he decided to put his own twist on them turning $60 into six-figure business. He didn't reinvent the wheel he took basic plain nachos and created a gold mine for himself. That's the grind and mentality young entrepreneurs and side hustle warriors have to develop. Everyone is not a natural born hustler, but over time you can learn to hustle at your own path. Running your own race.

But again, you're at the beginning of your life-changing journey. You have to change your surroundings this doesn't mean go out and buy a half a million-dollar house. No, you need to change what you do on a daily basis. Watching Facebook and IG first thing in the morning will not make you money. Unless you are watching other entrepreneurs or videos related to your business. Now changing what you eat and drink I am the last person on earth to tell someone what to consume but health is wealth in a way. You want your body and brain to match your bank account.

Lastly, but I think the most important change your crew. Now don't get me wrong if you are around very positive people who are on the same wave link then perfect grow with those people. But if your friends can only talk about clothes, celebrities and what's the newest tik tok dance get new friends period. You know who these people are and what energy they have around them change it ASAP. You need people who will challenge you and push you to be successful in your business. So, monitor relationships with the people in your life. Write down events and act accordingly. Remember no negativity in your journey for success. Adopting a millionaire mindset and work ethic your bank account will have no choice but to catch up w th you. The minute you choose to do what you really want to do, it's a different kind of life altogether.

"Do what you have to do, so you will be able to do want you want to do".

— *Denzel Washington*

Chapter 2

"Started from the bottom, now you're here"

The starting line is the craziest and most confusing point in your whole entrepreneur journey. But, I'm going to make this easy for you to navigate down the right road. If you are not a note taking kind of person no worries I'm not either. But in this chapter, you will need a notebook, memo recorder or napkin, something to capture the information and ideas. I have personally came up with hundreds of ideas for a new business but I would forget what I came up with the very next day because I didn't capture my thoughts. So, let's get started thinking about what kind of business you want to start. In reality there are only four types of businesses for entrepreneurs to enter into:

- Selling a product

- Providing a service

- Monetizing on social media

- Wholesale/ E-Commerce

An entrepreneur and side hustle warrior will fall into one or all four of these types of businesses. Looking at selling a product developing a new fresh product to offer to the public. There are a million products that are being sold across the world to improve people lives or style. I think the greatest example of a company with an incredible product that many people can relate to is FUBU. Starting with just a $20 ball cap FUBU turned into a billion dollar hip-hop culture fashion giant in the 90s. Daymond John CEO of FUBU and TV personality on shark tank was living in his mother's house when he developed FUBU and worked at Red Lobster waiting tables. I am not going to go deep into Daymond story but he is doing very well for himself. Looking at his story you can see he started from the bottom of the barrel and made moves to the top.

This is a great example that shows it doesn't take a lot of money to develop a product but more of sweat equity and somewhat unique product to sell to customers. So in your notes write down five to ten product ideas that make sense. How would that product improve someone's life or daily routine? Is this a product that customers can purchase more than one time? Answering these questions helps you build the product idea information profile.

The next section is providing a service to a client. For entrepreneurs and side hustle warriors this business field is very wide open. Great service speaks for itself that is your selling point. People love great service and eye to detail. But you still have to start the business up just like you would a product. The sweat equity has to be on hundred to build that client list. Answer the same questions, How will your service help someone's life or daily routine? Is this a service a client can use over and over again? Write these answers down so you can see what direction you can go down.

But the new and creative way to make money to monetize a product or service even yourself, is on social media. The idea is market on all major social media apps. Since 2010 having a social media is a great hustle if it is setup the right way. The applications are set so you can sell anything you want. But it's not that easy that's why a lot of universities business schools started a social media business course. I know I'm going to give you the information for this book how you use it that's up to you. The first thing you have to clean your timelines out from junk and crazy post that's not related to your business. Second, using hash tag will boost the post and reach people you wouldn't normally reach. Lastly, post everyday something related to your business or tell people that you're even starting a business. Make the public aware of what you are doing is very important. Remember social media is a free tool to use to your advantage. Yes, they have ads you can pay for to help boost your product it's up to you and your pockets.

Now, there is one more business type that you may fall into if setup right you can be very successful without doing the hard labor part. I call it the middleman effect think of it like this person "A" is ooking for a pair of Jordan 1s rare he can't find them. Ferson "A" post in a group chat or where-ever you see it. Now, you know that person "C" is selling Jordan 1s for $350 new condition. So, you contact person "A" tell them I can get the Jordan 1s for you but will cost $550. See you just made $200 without even touching the procuct this arrangement is very normal, you working as a broker. Ok, your homework for this section is to figure out what type of business you want to start. Most important write it down. I have provided a page so you can think and write at the same time.

"Success isn't always about greatness. It's about consistency. Consistent hard work will lead to success. Greatness will come"

— Dwayne "The Rock" Johnson

Chapter 3

C.R.E.A.M

When you think of C.R.E.A.M most people will say oh Wu Tang "Cash Rules Everything Around Me" or you are just simply craving for ice cream. But in my world as an entrepreneur and side hustle warrior C.R.E.A.M means "Creating Revenue Even After Mistakes." I am going to get straight to the point, this is to help you still plan to make revenue if you make a mistake. The key word here is "if". Why if, because the book is designed to help you navigate around or handle mistakes in the beginning stages of your business. Now, to be honest mistakes may still happen with things out of your control. But that's why we plan for ssues that may happen from beginning to end. You may say how in the world am I going to plan for something that didn't happen yet?

Good question, that's why you have to know your product and service like the back of your hand, your product fails, how can you still keep the business while the issue is being resolved? Or whom would you have working on a client site fixing an issue in a timely manner. But the main thing is to have C.R.E.A.M coming in while you correct the issue. A great example true story how tracing money can go really wrong my first business a very good leaning experience. First, don't ever buy clothes from China because the sizes are not equal to America. I jumped in the world of drop shipping. I knew nothing about it researched for about two hours that's it. I thought I was a professional until my very first order was placed. All I can do now is shake my head laugh because I got through it without any major scares. So, a very nice lady who worked with my wife at the time placed an order for a pretty sweater I had on the website. She ordered a 2X because even on the website I had on every product item may run smaller order bigger size. Ok, the first strike the shipping took 3 weeks 22 days before she received the product that's not good. Second strike the product was so small it could fit her 7-year-old daughter. This was bad all around on the very first order. So, we provided the customer with a full refund but when the same issues happened on the second and third order I said nope. Shut the entire website down and went back to the drawing board. Because you see the first thing you don't want to do is lose money in your new business. The money that's going out of your business should be for operational reasons not refunds to customers. So, the point to this story don't be like me

Back to the book, you will need to pick a business that even in failure you make revenue. I know you just looked at the book with a side eye, saying to yourself Jeremy you said you don't want us to fail. You want us to fall into that 80% of businesses that are successful. That is all a very true statement, but failure is not about your business going under. Failure is about making changes to your goals that can't be reached. For example, if your goal is to promote your business everyday every hour on the hour but you only promote for one day. Then that's a failure. You didn't reach your goal, but the business is still running. You would just have to get focused and set a goal that can be reached. Now, looking at it from another point of view this example shows someone who failed because they never got started. We all know this person who talk and talk about starting a business and actually have great ideas. So, everyday they say my goal is to start my business plan right after my TV shows go off. They failed to get started. One day turns into weeks, into years, sometimes into never. So again don't look at failure as it's over. Look at failure as the best teacher you will ever have.

Look at Michael Jordan arguably the greatest basketball player to play the game. He was cut from his freshman team in high school. Failing to make the team pushed his drive to be the best because he said he never wanted to feel failure like that again, ultimately of course making the team the following year and everybody knows what happened after that. He went on to win the National Championship UNC, 6 NBA Championships and is now inducted into the hall of fame. Keep in mind I am a die heart Detroit Pistons fan through and true. We don't like the Bulls, Lakers, and

Celtics but mainly we can't stand MJ. But I can respect his story and drive to be one of the greats. If you notice I use sports as a way to translate my message to my students and readers. But the message I want you to take from that story is failure is not an option. Starting this business can and will be a life changing event for you and yours. Don't let your failures or a roadblock detach your future in business and in life.

"Everyday I need you to set new goals
for yourself"

— Robert Smith

Chapter 4

"Working 9 to 5"

Recreating the famous line from the movie terminator "I'll be back" well I think that was the terminator! Anyway, the statement stands strong and true. You will be back day after day after day. Work until you retire in at 65 years old I think now it's 75 years old. But most people master plan is to work long hours for just ok pay. When you define the difference in work personalities that have it's pretty simple. There are only two kinds to define, you have one person who love everything about their job. Then you have the other who sits on the edge of the bed thinking about calling off. Practicing playing sick because they don't like their job at all, hate everything about it especially the people. I know you can relate to one of these people either you love your job or you don't. Both can resonate to becoming an entrepreneur and side hustle warrior but they can also crash and burn. Let's look deeper into this. Here are a couple of examples so you can picture and relate to one of them.

Example 1: Tracy graduated at the top of her class from the University of Miami. Now she works in an entry-level position for a large insurance company managing corporate accounts. Tracy likes what she is paid to do, but the long hours don't equal to her salary. The managers at the company notice Tracy's hard work and decides to have a meeting to talk about her future with the company. More like a yearly performance meeting for validation to receive a raise. Tracy heard about the raises amounts from another employee, their comments were not very good. But, Tracy knows she works harder than all of the other clerks hands down not even close. So, in the meeting Tracy's manager talks about how she brings great value to the company since she started. He said the clients like her professionalism when she's handling their account's.

He went on and on that meeting lasted about 35 minutes. They both shook hands and went back to work. Tracy felt great thinking about what her raise was going to be. Tracy talking to her self this money will help fix up my house or I can finally get a new car. Tracy has been taking the bus and riding her bicycle for 3 years. The next following week she wakes up early to check her bank account. She had to wipe her eyes then she logged out and back in. Tracy was so heartbroken that her pay didn't change and she only received a two percent raise. She still went to work feeling down and questioning her performance. What did I do or say? One of Tracy's co-workers was in the cubicle across the aisle, saw Tracy with her head down. She asked her what is wrong? Tracy replied, "I don't think I'm doing a good job here." The co-worker said, "what do you mean you are the best employee here." Tracy said I guess! But just got a two percent raise. The co-worker looked at her smiled and replied, "sweety everybody on the floor got a two percent raise good or bad." The co-worker continued to provide details to Tracy. She said, "I have been here 7 years and always received a two percent raise." Tracy looked at her like you're not a very good employee and you don't go the extra mile for the client. The co-worker laughed she said, "I used to have that getter done spirit you have now, it changed after my second year here and my second two percent raise." So, Tracy asked the co-worker what did you do? Did you start to look for another job? The co-worker said "no, absolutely not I love my job and my clients love me." The co-worker explained you could make money and have something for yourself outside of the company. Tracy looks up at the ceiling started brainstorming on just the idea of having her own business. The co-worker jokingly said, "make money legally no young girl hanky-panky." They both laughed Tracy said, "that's not my personality" and she stated she is scared of prison. So, that was her start to a journey and future of entrepreneurship. Her great company forced her to open her eyes to other options. But remember this is a side hustle warrior move because Tracy is keeping her 9 to 5.

Example 2 is definitely different then Tracy situation. Chris is a hard working man blue-collar handy man by trade. He can fix just about anything in a house. He didn't go to college or attend a fancy school. Chris graduated from high school and started his life. He had a business before the age of 17 after his high school counselor signed him up for the local trade school. He learned how to fix everything from the roof to the hardwood floors. But his biggest thing he learned was to turn his skill into a successful business. His instructor told him to save his money and pay yourself first every time he completed a job. Chris listened to the instructor and started saving small amounts like $10 off every job raising the amount over time. His goal is to buy a house and a new shop to grow his business even more. After 10 years of saving and working Chris saved over $400,000 in his bank account. His business is growing like wild flowers and his family is enjoying their new house. This example is pretty simple Chris was not well educated but he used the skill that he learned to capitalize a profitable business. This shows you no matter what level of education you have business is based on your hard work and willingness to learn. Chris started a business before 17 but his instructor opened his eyes to ownership. So think about this, until you provide a service like handyman

Chris to upscale your own business and have employees, you are just an employee in your own business.

Albert Einstein once said, "Try not to become a man of success. Rather become a man of value" very powerful quote. In this day and time I would state "man or woman" but the quote is very true. In business your value is very important but remember know you're worth.

The last example is my own situation, it is my very own story. I ran my business as a side hustle for years. Detailing a client vehicle on the weekend and counseling future business owners' everyday. Still working my day job in IT in the corporate arena for 8 years. I liked my job but I felt like Tracy my value was a lot more than they were giving me. But I was comfortable getting a paycheck every two weeks. That comfortability is what kept me there all those years, it was my security blanket. Look at it this way for an entrepreneur it is the one set back. Yes you're making money but your time is mainly at your 9 to 5. How are you able to build your business? Every person in the world has the same 24 hours 1440 minute and 86400 seconds, as an entrepreneur you can't waste any time. So, for 2 to 3 years, I kept saying I am going to go full time with my business but never actually pulled the trigger on doing it. Well on May 31, 2020 Covid-19 forced me to make a change in my life and business. I was terminated, laid off from my job, well my whole IT department was let go on a Zoom call. When it happened, it felt like freedom. I was so happy I did a dance in the middle of my living room that's funny because I can't dance. As soon as I got off the Zoom call, I went into full entrepreneur planning mode and let's just say I will never work for anyone else. Since being terminated I have doubled my clientele in the detailing business. I have started a new hot sauce business with some crazy flavors naming the business Team Brooks Savage Sauce. We also provide business counseling as an online class. But we have several new programs that are coming down the pipeline. I wanted to use my own story because if I wasn't forced out, I would have never developed the courage to know I was built for this. Trust me I knew I was going to be ok. But it took a tragedy to push me out the window to know I will land on my feet. A lot of future entrepreneurs are at that mentality that they will not step out on faith with their business because the feeling of a weekly check is also their security blanket. I can truly understand the feeling 100% its all fear.

Nelson Mandela said in a speech "Courage is not the absence of fear, but the triumph over it. The brave man is not he who does not feel afraid, but he who conquers that fear."

"Your self-worth is determined by you. You don't have to depend on someone telling you who you are."

— *Beyonce*

Chapter 5

"Thinking of a master plan"

Now to the meat and potatoes, business plan talk, working on the master plan is what I call it. A business plan is like planning your newborn child first day home from the hospital. Your business is your baby, so you have to make a decision during your planning to go in the right direction. Ok, since this is one of the most important part of running a successful business, we are going to look at this chapter in deoth. You will know how to write a business plan and explain everything within the plan to investors but really you write the plan for yourself. The plan is a blue print for your business. So, let's get started. I am not a teacher this will not be boring, but you are going to learn today (a little joke). Let's get to work I am pretty sure everyone knows what a business plan is but many have no idea how to write one. Ok, let's take this step by step, section by section. Yes, business plans are broken up into multiple categories basically telling the reader a story about your business. There are two different types of plans you can write a very detailed one or you can create a one-page brief summary with small but detailed information.

There are seven major sections of a business plan most entrepreneurs create to complete the plan listed below from the SBA.gov.

Traditional business plan outline:

- **Executive summary**
- **Company description**
- **Market analysis**
- **Organization and management**
- **Service or product line**
- **Marketing and sales**
- **Financial projections**

These are the main categories most business plans have to complete the plan. But of course, you can add more sections like Funding request to fully tell your story aligning your business on the right track. Financial institutions and private investors will need this section to view if you will be able to run and pay the money back. Let's look at each section in depth to clearly understand what each section provides the reader of the plan. The reader should be able to close their eyes and picture your business operation just by reading each section. Now, you most likely said I don't know the first thing about writing a business plan. How in the world do I do it? No fear you can use a formatted business plan template or you can find really good templates on SBA website. Google "business plan template" but do not copy the template information, the point is the help to structure your vision onto paper. I always say a well-structured business plan is not just for the readers but also mainly for yourself to stay on track within your business. Ok, now looking at each section starting with "Company descriptions" I know you're reading that correctly executive summary is the first one on the list but it will be the last section you will complete. Keep in mind I have written numerous business plans all of them are totally different from the start because your business changes over time, never stays the same. Back to the company description it is exactly what the title said give a complete description of your business. These sections should have these key points in it: your mission statement, management and business document classification. That's why I have provided a note section for you to write in your first company description. Now listen, this information gives you the opportunity to brag about your business and what makes it so great. Treat these sections just like if you were talking to a friend telling them all about your business the excitement needs to be visible to the reader.

Ok, the next section you may want to work on is the organization and management within the business. This section is easy to complete and honestly you have already put this information in the company description. But this is where you will go more in depth telling the readers what job is for what. For example, you are the owner maybe even manager of the business until you are able to hire someone to take over the daily duties. So, you will need to write down what is your experience in the industry. But, look you don't have to hold a MBA for your business to be successful just the grind and understanding. Meaning your business can't be your first day on a job you have to produce a little bit of experience, you have to be able to talk about the industry you enter into. Also, add who will be on the management team and what experience they bring to the table.

Now we need to look at the market analysis and marketing sales. This is where you tell the reader who is your target market. Your demographic. How will they see your product or service? Also, why your product or service is better than everybody else's? Those are the questions that need to be answered to complete this section. But mainly what will be the budget for the whole marketing campaign. So, this brings us to the financial part, this is where you add up every nickel dime and penny to make the business make sense. But, honestly you can start some businesses with very little money. If you have a home run business plan and no money in the bank you still get it started. But in your business plan your financial projections have to be set in the past, present, and future. For example, if you are starting a new car dealership business. In your me plan you would calculate how much it cost you to operate the dealership. How much profit will you make off each car? When you do the math the formula is simple. The formula is "total revenue - total expenses = profit." The profit is calculated after the overhead is deducted.

Now you can work on the last section Executive Summary. Keep this section straight to the point tell the reader how incredible your business is and why they need to invest in you. But you would mainly repeat a very short summary of everything you previously wrote in each section.

That is it! Everything you need to know about writing a basic business plan. Now, of course you can write an over the top plan but honestly most readers only going to look at the first three lines of the plan. Some investment meetings last 3 minutes. You have 3 minutes to change your life.

"Have a plan. Have a step-by-step list of things to do to get to your goal. If you don't have that, it's hard to have faith in what you're doing."

— Nipsey Hussel TMC

Business Plan Notes: Use this section to structure your plan.

EXECUTIVE SUMMARY

_____

_____

_____

_____

_____

_____

_____

_____

_____

_____

_____

_____

_____

_____

_____

_____

_____

_____

_____

_____

_____

_____

_____

_____

_____

_____

_____

COMPANY DESCRIPTION

_____

_____

_____

_____

_____

_____

_____

_____

_____

_____

_____

_____

_____

_____

_____

_____

_____

_____

_____

_____

_____

_____

_____

_____

_____

_____

_____

_____

_____

_____

_____

_____

_____

_____

_____

_____

_____

_____

_____

_____

_____

JEREMY BROOKS

MARKET ANALYSIS

_____

_____

_____

_____

_____

_____

_____

_____

_____

_____

_____

_____

_____

_____

ORGANIZATION AND MANAGEMENT

SERVICE OR PRODUCT LINE

_____

_____

_____

_____

_____

_____

_____

_____

_____

_____

_____

_____

_____

_____

_____

_____

_____

_____

_____

_____

_____

_____

_____

_____

_____

_____

_____

_____

MARKETING AND SALES

_____

_____

_____

_____

_____

_____

_____

_____

_____

_____

_____

_____

_____

_____

_____

FINANCIAL PROJECTIONS

_____

_____

_____

_____

_____

_____

_____

_____

_____

_____

_____

_____

_____

_____

_____

_____

Chapter 6

"Run your own race"

When you jump into the entrepreneurship world everything will seem like it's moving really fast and quick. But you have to run your own race at your own speed. One thing to remember is entrepreneurship is a long marathon not the 100-yard dash. These are life changing moves you are making. So, now that you have your business plan wrote out and finalized you should now know which direction your business will go. Setting up your business will be tiring and rewarding at the same time. Ok, let's go through the checklist of steps before you launch on the first day. Let's step back for a second think about when you started researching and dreaming about your business. You may have people come to you telling you why are you wasting time starting this business? Followed by the statement; I have a co-worker in this investment group, he is making crazy fast money on cash app. It's not a pyramid scheme its for real. This happens everyday to people looking for a quick buck. Just keep in mind this is not real the whole thing is a new age pyramid scheme. When people invest in a product or business it is an even split between all involved parties. You should never have to recruit people to double your money that sounds crazy. So, remember if someone tells you its fast and easy money, run away fast. Think about your money like a seed, it can feed your business to help it grow. The message is don't waste your money on dumb things. Here is a quick story about myself working three jobs and running my business at the same time. Listen, entrepreneurship is not for everyone but ownership can create generational wealth for your family. Yes, this book is about starting your own business, but you can also purchase land or invest in stocks and bonds. I have already started my incredible investment portfolio before I retire. This means I have to do a lot of research and saving. Money is really important to my operation, without it no business can make serious moves. Ok, I have a confession, back when I was attending Clark Atlanta University, like most teenaged college students I was smelling myself thinking I knew it all. This was back in 2001 during spring break the school hosted a bus trip from Atlanta Georgia to Daytona Beach. I think the trip was $300 or $400 per person I don't really remember because I didn't have the money to go anyway. I had $52 in my bank account and too much time on my hands. So, a couple of my friends went on the bus trip the campus was dead. After they left at the last second about 6 of us decided to drive down to Daytona Beach. But we had one problem no one had a car. I said its Atlanta, we should be able to find a rental car place in the hood for cheap. We did, the place was called "rent a wreck." Six college students packed in a Ford Taurus headed to Daytona Beach. Keep in mind now I only have $22 in my bank account after paying for the rental car.

But by the grace of God, we actually made it down to Daytona Beach driving in the middle of the night. This is where I get dumber because my tax return hit my account that same day I didn't even know. I knew I had $22 to my name for the weekend, but nope I was rolling with $446 in my account. I went crazy for a broke college student it felt like a million dollars. The next day we all went down to the beach because BET/MTV was doing Spring Bling beach party. We seen people standing around playing a card game, it looked very easy. I thought to myself I just need to pick the right card, I have never seen this before it was new to me. I tried it out, bet $10 I won double my money. I went up on the bet $20 I won double my money again. I said one more time $100 I loss, money was gone in seconds. People looked at me shook their heads my boy said they got you. He said, "they scammed you. You never heard of "three card monte?" Since that day I said I will never waste money again. I learned my lesson, great trip and adventure. We also had a bad encounter with TI at the hotel where there was a little knife involved. We saw Missy Elliott and Timberland also Cam'ron. It's more to that story but I will leave it for the next book.

Back to the business let your money be the water needed to feed the seed of your business. Meaning don't waste your time and money. The crazy thing people will say it's not a pyramid scheme, your 9 to 5 is a pyramid scheme, which is true. Business is based on a pyramid structure meaning every bus ness has; a CEO/ Owners, Managers, and Employees. Look at the chart to get a better understanding. Salaries are based on the size of the company just an estimate start pay.

CEO/Owner	Responsible for making operational decisions that benefits the company. Salary range $300,000 - $1billion
Manager	Answers to the CEO. Making sure the operation is running smoothly. Salary range $40,000 - $100,000
Assistant Manager	Answer to the Manager. Work under the manager. Salary range $30,000 to $60,000
Employees	Answers to everyone (CEO, Manager, and Assistant Manager) Work on most of the daily business for the company. Salary range $25,000 to $35,000

If you notice something different about each column take a good look. Yes, the salaries are different but there is one thing that is incredibly common in each business. Who is at the top? What is the eye popping difference? Right, the CEO answers to no one in the business. Look at the company 9 to 5 where you work at now. How many times have you ever talked to the CEO? Have you ever seen the CEO working getting their hands dirty? Do you even know who the CEO is? Like I mentioned before I've worked in different industries and have seen different CEOs and Owners. The one thing they had in common was I didn't see a lot of them. When I worked at a body shop car repair, as a teenager the owner would stop in once a week smoking a cigarette talking to everybody. But when I worked in the corporate world the CEO would visit once a year or not at all. When I worked at Cisco Systems before I never seen the CEO for Cisco didn't even know who he or she was honestly I didn't care. I was an employee at the bottom of the pyramid. So as you can see the pyramid for business always lead to the top. In business this is very legal. Even in families homes as the pyramid structure is there (grandparents, parents, and children). So as a business owner your mind set has to be set at the top of the pyramid. This doesn't mean you look down on your employees, it means you over see everything and everybody.

Table A – Showing the ownership Pyramid

Business Owner
Manager
Employees

Table B – Showing the owner working in every level

Business Owner
Business Owner/Manager
Business Owner/Employee

"Don't let anyone work harder than you do."

— Serena Williams

Chapter 7

"Dust your shoulders off"

Imagine you just got through your first fourth quarter in your business. Like most rookies n any sport your first year was a roller coaster but the best ride of your life. Just think about Kobe Bryant's first game as a Laker he scored 0 points in fact in his first 5 games he scored a total of 18 points and 3 rebounds. Think about this, Kobe Bryant was one of the best basketball players on earth some may argue he passed Jordan. But Kobe's first year was up and down but his drive pushed him to be a star. I am using Kobe as a perfect metaphor because of his alter ego "black mamba." He transforms into this mamba mentality meaning a constant quest to be the best version of one's self. Well you may say that was great for Kobe, how would that help me? You have to focus in on the mentality of the mamba, fearless and wellness to get the job done. Because as an entrepreneur and hustle side warrior, being fearless will help through the rough days or weeks. Use your first year as a try-out to see what works and what you need to change. The first year is the opportunity to see what flows perfectly in the business system. A lot of people fail in the first year because they never have a plan, or they don't have the business structure set up correctly not allowing benefits for the business to be received such as taxes and business credit. We are going to go deeper in Business credit in the next chapter. Here is a good activity you can try out. The goal is to visualize what year 1, 3, and 5 would look like before even starting the business. But the challenging part is you have to do the good and bad. Creating root causes and solutions that would keep the business growing.

"The most important thing is to try and inspire people so that they can be great in whatever they want to do"

— *Kobe Bryant 8:24*

Chapter 8

"I'm not a Businessman ... I'm a Business, man"

Thinking about business credit, there are different ways you can access credit through your business. Keep in mind business credit is tota ly different than your personal credit. Yes, sure they both use a credit score and they both report to the crecit agencies. Now, just because I use the word credit don't mean it is ball out time, it is actually the complete opposite. Business credit can be the heart beat of your business. The beauty of the whole structure of business credits set is that it allows your personal credit to be totally separate. Think about this you can have the worse personal credit score ever, but have incredible business credit. This is called the before DUN score. For example, Let's talk about Donald Trump. The man filed for bankruptcy four times but still managed to secure over 11 million in business credit.

We are going to look deep into business credit. How can you navigate your business using just business credit? Also, what are the benefits to using business credit?

Ok, let's define business credit in the mind of an entrepreneur. Just think about debt as a good tool. The problem people combine or think personal credit is the same as business credit. So, first throw the personal credit mind set out of the window. Business credit is on a 100-point scale not 800 like personal credit. Business credit is registered under the business Dun and Bradstreet number. You can receive this number two different ways. You can go online manually complete the registration. But you can also receive a number by opening an account with a vendor. The vendor will check your DUN number if you don't have one it will be automatically created for you. Of course, your business credit comes with an incredible, large level of responsibility. Vendors will trust that you will pay your bill on time.

Here is an example that will help you understand. Tim has a cleaning company, for years he would buy his supplies from the local big box store. After talking to his best friend Mike who is also a business owner, Mike told him to open an account with Grainger to get his supplies. Tim signed up online and placed his first order for cleaning supplies. Grainger set him up for a Net 30 account. Business credit account will be setup in three different payment terms (Net 30, Net 60, and Net 90) "Net 30" means you have 30 days to clear the balance.

So as a business owner the fastest way to build the credit is to place an order then pay it off within 10 days. Keep in mind it's hard to track everything that comes in. So, hire you a very good CPA or Tax attorney. Write down a list of the steps to get the business validated and operating as a business. Lastly, put yourself on the payroll this will help with taxes and to balance your books. Now this don't mean pay yourself a ridiculous salary. No keep it between a good range and stick to that amount. Do not I repeat do not dip in the business account to buy silly things. Remember if you stay focused, watch your numbers, you will not stress over the money coming in and going out.

"It doesn't matter if a million people tell you what you can't do, or if ten million people tell you no. If you get one yes from God, that's all you need."

— *Tyler Perry*

Chapter 1

"Sky's the limit"

We are finally to one of my favorite chapters because this is when you can think about the different limits you can go. In chapter 1, I asked you a couple of questions Why? and What? You should have a good answer to both questions. If you don't, please reread the book start with the introduction. I am a person who don't like wasting time because every second in my life I am one move closer to my goal. Listen this chapter is designed to show you that there are no limits. In business the owner doesn't have a salary, you can make $100,000 a month if you wish, of course with hard work it's not going to just come to you. But this chapter is also designed for the working person to show them that every 9 to 5 has a salary cap. From a doctor to a teacher they are all told what the pay will be. Most of the time you are going to be under paid for your skill level. That's just how the corporate world works pay less save more. No, I'm not talking about the shoe store but it's the same way of thinking. I will always motivate anyone who have a 9 to 5 to start a business or side hustle even if you make $100,000 a year "salary cap" which after taxes is really $72,154 a year still good money. But the owner is paying you 100k they are making over a million easy no salary cap and they get most of their million dollars by paying the same amount of taxes you pay. Most millionaires only pay $10,000 or less in taxes. Why? Because we can write just about everything off for the year. It's a chess game that the true masters take advantage of with good planning. It's a documented fact Jeff Bezos company Amazon paid $0 in taxes in fact they received a return on the company taxes for the physical year. This is very legal and is why you need to have a great not just a good CPA or Tax attorney to navigate through the laws.

Let's review the steps you need to do to make 20 to 30 thousand dollars extra income a month or year it depends on your efforts. Yes, this is very possible remember we talked about it in chapter 1 preparing your mind, body, and soul to become an entrepreneur. Again, think about yourself as an athlete the star on the team who has to take the team to glory. But the only way your team will win the championship you have to perform on a higher level. Michael Jordan and Tom Brady are the best players in their respectable sport. You have to take on that warr or mentality as a leader and champion. So, get yourself mentally ready to enter this entrepreneur world. Ok, in chapter 5 we talked about thinking of a plan, working on your business plan. This is the blueprint for your business and the wheel that will drive the business forward. Just remember your business plan may change multiple times before you are happy with the plan. Because understand your business may change so the business plan will change also. Take the time to research the type of business plan you want to write. Also, practice presenting your business plan to family and friends so when you are ready to go to the bank or going to an investor's meeting you will be ready.

The next step we talked about in chapter 8, applying for business credit and how to use business credit and debt to your advantage. Covering how to get a DUN number and how you will get invoiced (Net 30, Net 60 and Net 90). Important thing to remember debt is good, but of course paying your vendors bills off will keep you in good standing. But I think the final through for this entrepreneur and side hustle warrior's handbook is, a starting guide to motivate your decisions moving forward and successfully doing it in every way. Success is the hand of the beholder meaning you control your own success by the sweat and knowledge. Remember to learn and teach the up coming future entrepreneurs in the world.

"Making your mark on the world is hard. If it were easy, everybody would do it. But it's not. It takes patience, it takes commitment and it comes with plenty of failure along the way."

— *Barack Obama 44*

Acknowledgments

I think this was the toughest section to write because I have so many people to acknowledge on my journey in life. I learned something from someone everyday from different walks of life.

First thing I want to thank God for providing me with the strength to handle every challenge I have taken on. I was never afraid because I know my Lord and Savior was always with me.

Here we go this might be funny maybe a tear-jerker I don't know what direction I may go. Honestly, I maybe all over the place, just know this is coming from the heart. Let's start with Tenesha Brooks my beautiful wife, this woman is my backbone for everything in our house. I love this woman from the moon and back. She is the only person who can give me a headache then rub my head after. I am honored to share my life with you. Thinking about my kids, and how great they are handling this thing called life.

First my two oldest sons Stevie and Dannie. I have watched them both go from little boy's and transform into grown men who take care of their business. I have raised them to be respectful and hardworking men, the only thing I can say is they are definitely living up to everything I taught them. To my daughter Nevaeh, she's a female mini me. It is crazy how much she thinks like me. But this little girl is God's gift to the world because whatever she does in her life it is going to make a major impact changing people lives. Now to the youngest my baby boy Ethan. His uncle Duan calls him MC Brain. His IQ is on genius level for real and it scares me because he is 8 going on 38. The future architect can build anything out of Legos. My mother and father shoot without you two I wouldn't be here writing this crazy long thank you speech.

My sisters, I have shared a home with you two for half my life Chauna and N'jeri. I love you both for protecting me and abusing me like big sisters supposed to do. To my auntie Rozita Smith for having me over at her house every other weekend. I loved it over there that's when kids played outside. My uncle Vaughn for always talking to me about life in his own way. My bother in law Duan, I love that dude he needs his own show or podcast.

My bother and sisters from another Mother Jamar, Chann and Crease love you all like my blood sisters.

Now to my uncles and aunts on my dad side, love you guys'. My big family the Brooks family understand that's a lot of typing. To my cousins I have way too many to name on both my mother side and father side like a tribe. But I love you all.

To my boys my bothers my homies Greg "GP", Djbril "Bril" my CAU crew, D Winburn "Big Marty", Danny Boy my Batcave crew. My old co-workers Steven, Sterling and Trevis thank you for the support and guidance. A special thank you to my publishing team Steward Publishing great job. Lastly to everyone whoever supported any of our businesses thank you.